Colette Bryce

The Whole
& Rain-domed
Universe

PICADOR

First published 2014 by Picador
an imprint of Pan Macmillan, a division of Macmillan Publishers Limited
Pan Macmillan, 20 New Wharf Road, London N1 9RR
Basingstoke and Oxford
Associated companies throughout the world
www.panmacmillan.com

ISBN 978-1-4472-6343-2

9 8 7 6 5 4 3 2 1

A CIP catalogue record for this book is available from the British Library.

Printed and bound by CPI Group (UK) Ltd, Croydon, CR0 4YY

Visit **www.picador.com** to read more about all our books
and to buy them. You will also find features, author interviews and
news of any author events, and you can sign up for e-newsletters
so that you're always first to hear about our new releases.

for Bev Robinson

Like many inveterate travellers,
he was attached to his starting point
by a powerful piece of elastic

Graham Robb, *Rimbaud*

it is joy to be hidden but disaster
not to be found

D W Winnicott

Contents

The Whole & Rain-domed Universe

White

I stepped from my skis and stumbled in, like childhood,
knee deep, waist deep, chest deep, falling
for the sake of being caught
in its grip.

It was crisp and strangely dry and I thought: I could drop
here and sleep in my own shape, happily,
as the hare fits
to its form.

I could lie undiscovered like a fossil in a rock
until a hammer's gentle knock might
split it open; warm
and safe

in a wordless place (the snowfall's ample increase),
and finally drift into the dream of white
from which there is no
way back.

I placed myself in that cold case like an instrument into velvet
and slept.

Derry

I was born between the Creggan and the Bogside
    to the sounds of crowds and smashing glass,
by the river Foyle with its suicides and rip tides.
    I thought that city was nothing less

than the whole and rain-domed universe.
    A teacher's daughter, I was one of nine
faces afloat in the looking-glass
    fixed in the hall, but which was mine?

I wasn't ever sure.
    We walked to school, linked hand in hand
in twos and threes like paper dolls.
    I slowly grew to understand

the way the grey Cathedral cast
    its shadow on our learning, cool,
as sunlight crept from east to west.
    The adult world had tumbled into hell

from where it wouldn't find its way
    for thirty years. The local priest
played Elvis tunes and made us pray
    for starving children, and for peace,

and lastly for 'The King'. At mass we'd chant
    hypnotically, *Hail Holy Queen,*
mother of mercy; sing to Saint
    Columba of his *Small oak grove, O Derry mine.*

*

We'd cross the border in our red Cortina,
    stopped at the checkpoint just too long
for fractious children, searched by a teenager
    drowned in a uniform, cumbered with a gun,

who seemed to think we were trouble-on-the-run
    and not the Von Trapp Family Singers
harmonizing every song
    in rounds to pass the journey quicker.

Smoke coiled up from terraces
    and fog meandered softly down the valley
to the Brandywell and the greyhound races,
    the ancient walls with their huge graffiti,

arms that encircled the old city
    solidly. Beyond their pale,
the Rossville flats – mad vision of modernity;
    snarling crossbreeds leashed to rails.

A robot under remote control like us
    commenced its slow acceleration
towards a device at number six,
    home of the moderate politician;

only a hoax, for once, some boys
    had made from parcel tape and batteries
gathered on forays to the BSR,
    the disused electronics factory.

      *

The year was nineteen eighty-one,
　　the reign of Thatcher. 'Under Pressure'
was the song that played from pub to pub
　　where talk was all of hunger strikers

in the Maze, our jail within a jail.
　　A billboard near Free Derry Corner
clocked the days to the funerals
　　as riots blazed in the city centre.

Each day, we left for the grammar school,
　　behaved ourselves, pulled up our socks
for benevolent Sister Emmanuel
　　and the Order of Mercy. Then we'd flock

to the fleet of buses that ferried us
　　back to our lives, the Guildhall Square
where Shena Burns our scapegoat drunk
　　swayed in her chains like a dancing bear.

On the couch, we cheered as an Irish man
　　bid for the Worldwide Featherweight title
and I saw blue bruises on my mother's arms
　　when her sleeve fell back while filling the kettle

for tea. My bed against the door,
　　I pushed the music up as loud
as it would go and curled up on the floor
　　to shut the angry voices out.

　　　　*

My candle flame faltered in a cup;
    we were stood outside the barracks in a line
chanting in rhythm, calling for a stop
    to strip searches for the Armagh women.

The proof that Jesus was a Derry man?
    Thirty-three, unemployed and living with his mother,
the old joke ran. While half the town
    were queuing at the broo, the fortunate others

bent to the task of typing out the cheques.
    Boom! We'd jump at another explosion,
windows buckling in their frames, and next
    you could view the smouldering omission

in a row of shops, the missing tooth
    in a street. Gerry Adams' mouth
was out of sync in the goldfish bowl
    of the TV screen, our dubious link

with the world. Each summer, one by one,
    my sisters upped and crossed the water,
armed with a grant from the government
    – the Butler system's final flowers –

until my own turn came about:
    I watched that place grow small before
the plane ascended through the cloud
    and I could not see it clearly any more.

Re-entering the Egg

Like some magnificent Swiss clock,
the house has been rebuilt
in the same position, in that Georgian street.
Tall and lean, it tilts towards us,
lists like a ship on rough seas
as it always did, only look (how clever!)
the front can be opened
with this small lever.

A tiny family fills the rooms.
In one, a wife is breathing fire,
genies whirling in the air.
In one, we hear the Strong Man's snores
rumbling under a mound of clothes
like a subterranean train.
In one, first floor, a spangled girl
enters in her diary: *I am headed for a fall*.
In one, girl-twins, conjoined
at the skull, freak themselves
to a pitch of shrieks, *A rat, I saw it! There!*
In one, a mermaid, washed up on the floor,
amber-lit in the notional glow
of a three-bar fire, strums a guitar,
hooks blonde hair behind one ear.
Like a baby bird re-entering the egg,
the smallest girl's soft breath
knits round her like a shell, like pearl,
where she's curled up sleeping
on the topmost bunk
of a creaking bed.

A television flickers blue
in another room
and a British voice reports the news
as smoke-rings loosen in the air, disperse,
and turfs collapse in the grate
beneath the glowing coal
in the ruptured chest
of the Sacred Heart.

Out of time, they go about their lives
unaware of our scrutiny.
Close it up. That's enough for now.

Hide-and-seek

You fold your body into wardrobes,
breathe the potent musk of mothball,
perfume, cedar and dust. Disturb
the tiniest silky moths in rigid
handbags, snappy-clasped, and squirm
when hand finds fur in the dark,
relieved to reveal a Cossack hat
or balding rabbit stole.
You lie flat under mattresses,
hold your breath, slink behind a door
or heavy drapes that close *shhhh*,
you wait. Expert as a murderer,
you clock each chink in which a human
body might be quick-concealed:
squeeze into unlikely corners,
airing cupboard, cubby hole.
You shut the lid from deep within
the ottoman in mother's room,
its oriental satin. Its bellyful
of linen. You're small enough to store.
You're in the tallboy's outsized
bottom drawer, uncomfortable
on a bed of shoes, prepared
to wait, long as it takes. Watch out,
if you're too clever you might not ever
be found. England, say. Or adult life.
Seeker, let the search continue
into the secrets of that house.

Boredoom

The world was due to end next week
according to someone whose brother
had read Nostradamus. Magpies,
two for joy. Walk round ladders, *quick*,

touch wood. We mimed the prayer
of the Green Cross Code and waited,
good, at the side of the road. Blessed
ourselves when the ambulance sailed

by on a blue (our fingers, toes). Lay
awake in the fret of the night, thinking
about the Secret of Fatima, the four-
minute warning, the soft-boiled egg.

Our boomerang did not come back.
Frisbees lodged in the canopies
of trees forever, turning black.
I poked out moss from paving slabs

half-dreamingly, with an ice-pop stick,
then leapt at the looped rope of my name
called from a yard and dawdled home
trailing a strange tune on the xylophone railings.

The future lived in the crystal ball
of a snake preserved in alcohol
in my grandmother's attic. I looked,
on tiptoe, out through the lens

of the highest window; learned
the silver river's turn, the slogans daubed
on the ancient walls, the column of smoke
where something always burned.

The theatrical death of my maternal grandmother as revealed in a 1960s glitter globe

I give it a shake and look
again and spot
a pair of bunioned shoes
beneath a portly lady
at a table, contemplating
soup. The conversation
batted to and fro
with my mother
through the scullery door,
concerns the première
(on Broadway!) of
Philadelphia, Here I Come!
Before the lights
go out, and she hits
the boards, and a slow day
falters for a moment –
'Isn't it great', she shouts,
'to see a Derry man
getting on?'

Heritance

From her? Resilience. Generosity.
A teacher's gravitas.
Irish stew. A sense
of the ridiculous. High ceilings.
Neither a borrower nor a lender be.
Operatic plotlines.
Privacy.

An artery leading to the Spanish Armada,
a galleon dashed on the rocks at Moville, a sunken
grave, *se llama Hernando,*
black hair, despair,
a rose between the teeth.
Bullets. Books.
A low-toned voice.

An Antarctic explorer in a fur-lined hood
with the face of a pugilist
and a Russian wife in Brooklyn.
Bottles, half-full,
tilting in the ottoman.
O rhesus negative.
Tact, to a point.

Uncle Joe walking out of the Dáil in '22,
sold down the river.
An historical anger.
Stand-up piano.
Pilgrim feet.
A comic turn of phrase.
An iron constitution.

A horse appears,

led by a red-faced man,
hooves clopping on the tarmac.
You want so much
to sit up on that horse
that you race out in your socks
and, sure enough,
he swings you up
on its back
like being elected.
The street looms
at a tilt, a new slant
that riders of horses
have always known:
a foreignness.

*

You play with the stilts
when you get the chance,
silver poles like metal
crutches, footholds
you can raise
or drop. They lift
your view of things
by about one foot
and you advance
stiffly, synchronizing
arms and steps.

A woman asks
what they're made of;
you see the shape
of a word in your mind.
I-ron, you say, and she laughs
loudly. *I-ron, are they?*,
gentle mockery. You'd love
to try those stilts again.

The Analyst's Couch

I was not there when the soldier was shot, so I didn't see him
carried up the street and manoeuvred
through our propped front door.
Who took his weight, the women or the soldiers?
Blood, seeping into the cushions, dark brown stuff
like HP sauce, soaking thoroughly into the foam, the worn
upholstery of the enemy. *Laid out on the sofa*
of eternity, its faded tweed, its sag, its hoard
of household smells, fluff and pens, small change
and lost buttons. *Am I making this up?* Its animalness.
Paw-footed, it pads from the room, the soldier lying bleeding on its back.
No it doesn't.

Helicopters

Over time, you picture them
after dark, in searches

focusing on streets and houses
close above the churches

or balancing
on narrow wands of light.

And find so much depends upon
the way you choose

to look at them:
high in the night

their minor flares confused
among the stars, there

almost beautiful.
Or from way back

over the map
from where they might resemble

a business of flies
around the head wound of an animal.

North to the South

1

The map unfolded in the car
like a kite, a barely
controllable thing
to be wrestled, my father
overcome.

A giant's hands
might have practised origami,
a bird, or a boat
on which an impossible dream
might stay afloat.

2

A head through the window
on the driver's side.

Where have we come from?
Where are we going?

Eight little girls and a dog
spill out.

Aunty Máire was famous
for spelling out her name

P-Ó-G M-O T-H-Ó-I-N,
which they duly wrote down.

3

You are giving the vast Atlantic
to your father, bucketful
by bucketful, padding

to and fro on the damp strand
to store it at his feet
in a hole where

it only appears to vanish.

The Search

i.m. Jean McConville

All day we searched
for the wedding ring,
with a childish devotion
to the task. Marion,
in her postnatal sorrows
back at the house, twirling
a lock of her hair
over and over
and over, that faraway
look. *Poor Marion.*

Close to the dunes,
we sifted, dug. One
patch of sand soon merged
with another. Not a land
mark, not a post or rock,
the script of the beach
erased by the weather.
Our shadows loomed
on the lit strand,
conducting their own
investigation.

A small haul of items
amassed: a conch,
a twist of fisherman's
rope, the parched sole
of a shoe. Cloudy gems

of greenish glass; a picnic
cup, some patterned
cloth. At a loss,

we'd play, or bury
each other: feet,
knees, hips, chest; sand
in our hair, in our cuffs,
in the turn-ups
of our jeans, sand
in the creases of our skin,
as we scaled the heights
of the dunes and leapt
for dear life
into thin

air. Thirty years.
The coolness of that sand;
just coarse enough
to hold itself together
in the wind, but soft
like powdered gold
where our discarded
shadows had been thrown.

Magi

Joseph was the Famous Grouse,
and the Virgin Mary, the Babycham deer.
Standing in for the sheep and the ass
were the Black & White distillery terriers.

The shepherd loitering shyly with a lamp
was McEwan's Laughing Cavalier
and the followed star was a golden Harp,
the swaddling cloth, a Smithwick's towel.

Up on the walls where they hung all year
were Pio, Pearse and Johnny Walker
carrying whiskey, liberty and prayer;
gifts befitting an Irish saviour.

The Republicans

Their walls are like any other walls, muffled in layers of paste and paper.
Squares compete with a carpet's swirls. The room is a-clutter with
    adolescents,
children, ashtrays, dirty cups; a television's flash and jabber.

A man reclines in an armchair, dragged up close to the hearth, his feet
on the shelf. Glowing coals are banked with slack. Cooking smells waft in
from beyond the door. Two schoolgirls braid each other's hair.

Jesus opens his ruptured chest in a frame; in another, Jesus again
at an earlier age, in his mother's arms. In a third, a triptych in household
    gloss
depicts a map, a gun and a dove. *Ireland unfree shall never be at peace*

spelled out by sons in prison workshops. The republicans
rest their plates on their knees and gobble up their dinners, quickly.
Mince. Potatoes. Peas or beans. They light their fags and inhale, deeply.

Don't speak to the Brits, just pretend they don't exist

Two rubber bullets stand on the shelf,
from Bloody Sunday – mounted in silver,

space rockets docked and ready to go off;
like the Sky Ray Lolly that crimsons your lips

when the orange Quencher your brother gets
attracts a wasp that stings him on the tongue.

'Tongue' is what they call the Irish language,
'native tongue' you're learning at school.

Kathleen is sent home from the Gaeltacht
for speaking English, and it's there

at the Gaeltacht, ambling back
along country roads in pure darkness

that a boy from Dublin
talks his tongue right into your mouth,

holds you closely in the dark and calls it
French kissing (he says this in English).

Positions Prior to the Arrival of the Military

Mother (out for the count) has been carried
from the ring. *Ding ding!* we have a victor,

Father, who has vanished in a puff of smoke
from his pipe, to return in the small hours.

Sister has stepped from her sleeping body
and floats about unnoticed amongst us,

a dream she will later recount,
while brother, who sleeps on the ceiling

lately, gazes down like a Sistine cherub
with a lute, a stain spreading on the sheet

where he used to sleep before
he was safe. The screen in the corner

has much to offer: heart-warming stories,
Little House on the Prairie.

Satellite beams are connecting all this
with New York, Bangkok, the Moon (in theory).

You're climbing the banisters, monkeying up
through the house without the aid of stairs –

a test, if passed successfully,
that will save the world from nuclear meltdown.

Rat-a-tat-tat at the door and the dog
is going berserk. All hesitate

Hall Dream, Upended

The privacy glass
in the old front door

seems to resemble
rippling water,

water
dimpling under rain.

The only source of light
it pulls you forward

through a long-
hall gloom.

Like bones drowned
in the bottom of a well,

you reassemble,
swim.

The Brits

Whatever it was they were looking for, they liked
to arrive in the small hours, take us by surprise,
avoiding our eyes like gormless youngfellas
shuffling at a dance. My mother spoke:
a nod from the leader and the batch of heavy rifles
was stacked, *clackety-clack*, like a neat camp fire
under the arch of the hall table – her one
condition, with so many children
in their beds – each gun placed by a soldier
whose face, for an instant, hung in the mirror.
This done, the load of them thundered up the stairs,
filling our rooms like news of a tragedy.

Last night I dreamt of tiny soldiers,
like the action figures I played with as a child;
Fay Wray soldiers in the clumsy hands of Kong,
little Hasbro troopers in the massive hands of God.
I'd like to remove their camouflage and radios,
to dress them up in doll-sized clothes; little high street shirts,
jeans, trainers, the strip of ordinary sons and brothers.
I'd like to hand them back to their mothers.

Your Grandmother's House

The Toby jugs on her mantelshelf
are like a row of punters sitting at the bar,
red-cheeked, ever the worse for wear. In a mirror,
the Ulster Television News
or Scene Around Six: the latest murders.
Her call, weak, from the top of the stairs

(where *is* he?) *Son are you there?*, the stairs
creaking, footfalls, one by one. She steadies herself
in the unlit hall, enters and yes, she could murder
a nice cup of tea. A booth like in the bar;
a black banquette. The lilac light of the news
enfolds you in its trance, casts glints like a mirror-

ball around the room. In the convex mirror
fixed like a porthole to the wall, you stare
from far away, re-scaled, and watch the news
of a missing child as she frisks the shelf
for the spectacles she might have left in the bar
for goodness sake, but no, sure here they are. A murder

inquiry is what they want but is it a murder?
Nobody knows, with no body and the case a mirror
of the case last year (the talk of the bar)
where the child had been cowering under the stairs
all the while. She sets her saucer on the shelf
and settles back to wait for the news

headlines to repeat again. Your new
uniform prickles skin as you browse the murder
mysteries huddled fatly on a single shelf

and wait for your father to enter this mirror-
life in which he's come to live, in a room upstairs,
and take his place at the booth he calls 'the breakfast bar'

and make some awkward conversation. A bar
of chocolate. A soft drink. He'll angle for news
of your sisters, brother... *How's your mother?* You'll stare
ahead and fidget, What do *you* think? The murder
story cross-fades into the sports results and the mirror
holds a stranger, or some other self

who stares back blank as the child in the murder.
At the breakfast bar, as you knew
you would, you shelve this scene and exit the mirror.

A Clan Gathering

Dublin, 2009

Not a birthday only
but a clan gathering for Bríd.
Her poor old peerless eyes.
The young, peripheral.
The host, with his long jaw
and recreational shirt
distributing flutes of gold wine
to the old, the late, the rheumy-eyed,

who fill the bright reception room
with its view of the pool
and, further, the ocean; mingle,
awkward and sociable, polite
enquirers after each other's
links – a slight anxiety
to be leaves on the twigs of a
branch of the scheme of things.

They gather around
the family chart, unscrolled
on the sideboard, busily plot
themselves and theirs,
point and jostle, narratives
tumbling out of their mouths,
excitable flow of births,
deaths, accidents, marriages,

properties lost. What
it is all about, it seems,
is the simple multiplication
of the tribe. The ancients
lower themselves into chairs.
A ribboned child, somebody's
from England, picks out
phrases on the baby grand.

Bríd floats blindly through the guests,
immaculate in suit and shades.
She folds the hand of each in hers,
intent, intensely feeling her way,
heels clacking on the oak floor.
The hosts are oddly embarrassed
by their wealth, all modesty
and disconnect. In sepia,

the family heroes. Uncle Joe,
third from the left at the first Dáil,
his handsome face pure intellect...
A hand on an arm, smiles, guffaws,
a palpable text now almost visible
in the air; a set text, thick as a
swarm around the head-to-heads
and the have-you-met-yets.

I don't mention my lover,
how we have to invent
for ourselves a blank, unscripted
future; her guaranteed absence
from the diagram, the great
genetic military campaign,
and no one asks,
sensing a difference.

Outdoors, they spill onto several
levels, settle in groups and lean
on rails as if on the various decks
of a ship. United they stand
against death and difference:
my mother, who drew nine babies
from her body, as though
from out of a conjurer's cloak;

the low-key waiters, musicians,
caterers; toddlers chasing each other
through the legs; the North-
South divide, the Celtic Tiger,
unmet cousins, country farmers.
Time for a speech from the birthday girl!
A believer, she says, in genes,
genetic inheritance.

The sea's incredible equilibrium.
Imagine a tilt and the consequence.

The cypresses.

The four-by-fours in the drive.

Mammy Dozes

Mammy dozes in her chair.
Cushions packed in soft layers
are glowing with her heat.
Eighty years have lent her skin

a bruised look in composure,
a touch of purples
to the hollows, so Mammy dozing
resembles a boxer in defeat.

She could be anyone's mother,
any one of the old, alone
in living rooms throughout
this town, prey to junk mail,

meter readers, window cleaners,
priests. On *Deal or No Deal*
someone is winning, pounds
clocking up on screen.

In a peaceful corner of the
universe, with matching silver cars
in drives, magpies flashing
on the roof, Mammy sleeps.

Magic Eye

See him in the IRELAND baseball cap.
See her in a pair of too-large trainers
clowning down precipitous streets
to the special pub with the blacked-out panes
that no one else sets foot in, where only those
who have fallen through the cracks lie low.

They star in more scenes than you think,
take a look. Let your gaze relax
like Magic Eye, those pattern prints
where shapes might slowly surface. There
he lies: feel free to prod him with a toe,
put your mind at ease that, no,

he hasn't died. Inside his head
it is dark, a back road over the border
at night where a notional verge requires
great care and steps are perilous.
Their faces are breaking out of their faces,
livid red. When strangers clutch

her arm, concerned, or slap her cheek
and say her name, she sways to her feet
and stands before a hinterland
of rumour: kids in care, debts, abuse;
all of it called to explain why they kip
in boarded flats with rats or slumped

in a shop's entry, steaming where they lie.
They are up early, sit stunned
in a fizz of stars or flies and watch

the march of other lives to work,
managers raising shutters on the day,
bin men's sweep and clearance.

Their eyes, peeled in the morning sun,
though onion-raw, are looking in
towards some awful destination
to which each instinct is impelled
as needles drawn to north.
You blink, and find them gone.

Like you they lived their whole lives
in this town, their parts assured.
For that, perhaps, you should be glad
as you cross their path so hurriedly
in the shopping mall, and take your place
in line on the mirrored escalator, rising.

A Library Book

'Look after that, it's a library book.'
Tikki Tikki Tembo, the story of a boy
who fell down a well. The story of his brother
running to fetch the old man with the ladder.
Library books were special, hard-backed
ones that opened wide with creaks
like tomes that wizards possessed. Rest
your cheek against the cold slip-cover,
pictures vivid underneath. Run your fingertip
down the column of dates, stamped
for return by a kind librarian, each
corresponding to a child, a reader,
who carried it home to the order
or chaos of their lives and lost themselves
in the story. *Tikki tikki tembo no sa rembo*

chari bari ruchi pip peri pembo!
My sister and I could deliver his name in one breath –
a spell, or a poem by heart. Years later,
it took only one of us to start
and the words unfurled on cue
like a streamer. In student digs. By intercity
coach, I'd visit her in gas-fire flats
where she nursed the baby that arrived
before she was grown, where my sister
started falling, gradually at first,
into one particular dark. There was no
old man with a ladder, *climbing step
over step*. I go back to the book,
retrieved in an internet search, desperate
to remember what happened.

Jean

Because last night and because today,
you fix a drink to steady the shakes.

The soft cottage walls are swelling
into your cells, spores falling

freely, into the pit of tomorrow,
flammable, this life, this sorrow:

fountain pen; an old picture
in a cardboard frame, the face a crater.

Here's to the cruellest joke, Jean,
that it came too late, and never.

A little girl I knew when she was my mother

emerged from the pages of a bed

       from sheets the colour of old snow

crawled from the petals of the Weeping Rose

       from silks suffused with smoke

       and sweat

dragged her wings from a chrysalis

slipped from the folds of the Virgin's robes

uncurled her limbs
         like an opening fist
             ravelled
       free of the winding cloths

felt for the floor
       with the ball of her foot

       found a swirling-patterned carpet

raised a hand to her sleep-stiff hair

       breathed the ancient bedroom air.

There were black flags hanging from the houses

       rags fluttering in the breeze.

    *

Miles away, a dressing table.
Angels escort her ineffable steps

to rest on a piano stool,
all that is left of the instrument,

while under the seat, sheet music
hums to innocent childhood airs.

I see them floating in the triptych mirrors
the little girls I knew when they were my mothers.

They look down at their old hands,
jewelled rings screwed over knuckles.

There's a woman trapped in the centre of their body
that no one can remember, as if in amber.

They look down at their old hands
and cry, petals falling from their eyes.

(after Louise Bourgeois)

Signature

When I finally gave up and became my mother, I concentrated hard
and wrote myself a note for the teacher, kept
a steady hand
as I leant to the slant of her signature
in the style she had introduced to the schools of the North. I ripped
     a leaf
from her pad of Basildon Bond and found myself an envelope.
Dear Mrs Brophy... absent yesterday, because... Because
I had become my mother, the flourish
on that sloping *B*
was as natural to me as it was to my sister and co-forger who,
     ten years later,
when we dug out her flat in Morningside into black bin bags,
     after the breakdown,
had written on a card fixed in the nameplate on her door, *her name*
in that very same hand, the very same
flourish on the capital *B*, as natural to her as it was to me.

A Simple Modern Hand

1

The italic characteristics
begin to emerge:
slope,
economy of stroke.

They say compression
is the essence,
elements all
encased in the oval

n. u. v. a. o. x.
each confined
to its egg
or box. O mother,

what am I hankering after
with spidery hand,
signature pressure?
Do I mean

this tentative pen
to discover... What?
The torched
pages of a book?

Flakes of the truth
like black moths
at a grate?
A fire's cool erasure?

2

My mother's hand has been lost for good
like a maiden name, or a fingerprint
seared off by the thief who faked his own death
in a book – the buoyant cursive of her youth
with which she wrote to Alain – *amour!* –
the mythical Parisian whom all of our mothers
should really have married, but somehow let go,
to then fall prey to our no-good fathers
and all the predictable sinkers of a mother's
lot, on the sleeves, the spirit, and the heart.

3

One method of refining
a good italic hand
is by sandwiching *m*
between pairs of letters
mama – mama –
emem – emem –

denoting the bilabial
interrupted hum
with its stem and arches
and wavelike
momentum, bearing
on its shoulders
the pressure
of intention.

o is the governing shape,
the model, the oval
ever-elliptical hoop.

o is a nutshell,
Phoenician eyeball,
all-seeing, *o*
is the mouthshape
of surprise.

Extending the cross stroke
of an elegant *t*
will fluently link
to the letters that follow
ta – te – ti –
ti – toe – tum

and carry us on
to the slant
of the *h* or the shibboleth
haitch, a simple
single stroke,
alphabetically eighth

(and 'The Eighth'
incidentally,
was the title of a poem,
the only one she wrote).

e is the oval again,
the curled
most common vowel
in the English tongue,

the loop
tucked into
the centre
of the down stroke
which exits with the lift
to the terminal *r*.

From the *r*'s main stem,
the small, shoulder upstroke
should not be overdone;
if drawn too long
it may well interfere
with the letters that follow,

in this case none,
as we come to the end
of our word for today
and lift our pen
and our gaze
from where the ink
already dries.

4

With this transitional script
we mark a change.

5

We begin with a tiny corner
of a white page, edged
in bluish flame,

a fragment that increases
as the smouldering fringe expands,
paper forming in its wake,

neat lines of naïve script
– rounded letters,
circles adorning the *i*'s –

and the arc of flame moves on
like the widening
fingertip search of an area,

then narrows again
and peters away
revealing the newborn opposite

corner of the page,
an unburned sheet of paper.
Is it a letter? What does it say?

Wait, it is the first-burnt leaf
of a book, page 1, which now
takes its place on top

of the re-formed volume,
which slips into its cover
and is bound, for words

are indeed binding
(the reason for the burning
before all this),

and thus we return the word
to the world, and thus
we replace the heart

into the hearth
as we place the book
back into the hands

of its owner, only a child, a girl,
who smiles at us
and leans to her writing.

Asylum

(Iona)

Should a guest blow in from the north of Ireland,
    buffeted by the wind,

should the shadow of a cross, afloat on the water,
    mirror the flight of a pilgrim guest

pitching an effortful course through the buffeting gusts,
    this far from the north of Ireland;

should the pilgrim guest, whittled with hunger, depleted
    in reserves, lose altitude

and collapse on the stones of your own small island,
    beaten and worn,

stagger on the shingle, dragging magnificent wings like a cape,
    like an airman trailing his billowing silks,

you must lift this creature and carry it, gathered
    in your arms, over the field to the bothy,

and there, attend to its invalid needs
    for three consecutive days and nights,

during which time it may huddle in a corner, throat retracted
    into its ruff, stern as a cleric, gimlet-eyed,

yet gulping the silver herrings you proffer
    like pills, gaining strength, getting well,

till you walk with it back to the narrow beach, on day four,
    watch it take a run

and lift with the gawkiest of take-offs, creaking beats
    of its great span, neck and bill extended like an arrow

pointing the route to my old homeland
    – which is why I am so solicitous of your kindness –

ruling a line straight south to Malin Head
    and home, the sweet district of Ireland.

(After Adomnán's account of St Columba's prophecy of the heron)

Pisces

When the tide withdraws
like a jeweller's cloth
to reveal a mile
of glittering rocks,

what's not to love?
What's to stop
a human like you
in coat and gumboots

clambering out
to the furthest reach,
as near as dammit
to the sea floor?

What's to prevent
a human like you
from choosing a spot
on the planetary rocks

to live,
resolute as a limpet
sits tight
in its home scar?

The hermit crab
in its hermit shell.
You in your skull,
your pulsing fontanelle,

the North Sea
creeping up on you
again, fingertip
by fingertip, ready

to pounce

The Quiet Coach

Look, three loops from the silver locks
of my predecessor
whose journey southwards,
earlier today, was a textbook
reversal of my own.

In the weirder logic of a poem,
the woman is my mother
hurtling ever
backwards
through unseasonable snow.

She is steadily un-solving my Everyman
crossword, reinstating
each white space
as if in the wintry landscape
of her brain.

On arrival, all solutions
are undone. I bow my head
to the questions.

Acknowledgements & Notes

Acknowledgement is due to the editors of the following
publications in which earlier versions of some poems appeared:
*Atlanta Review, Causeway, Edinburgh Review, The Guardian,
Irish Times, Jubilee Lines* (Faber), *Magma, Matter 5, The Moth,
Poetry London, Poetry Review, Wake Forest Series of Irish Poetry* 3,
Wasafiri, Yellow Nib, Gift and *Shadow Script* (NCLA).
I am grateful to New Writing North for a Time to Write award
in 2011, and the Authors' Foundation for an Arthur Welton
award in 2013. Special thanks to Linda France, Martha Kapos,
Bev Robinson and Una Bryce for reading.

Several poems echo openings by writers and artists I admire,
specifically: 'Derry', Louis MacNeice; 'Re-entering the Egg',
Anne Sexton; 'Signature', Sharon Olds, and 'Mammy Dozes',
August Kleinzahler. 'A little girl I knew when she was my mother'
borrows its title from an artwork by Louise Bourgeois.
The Keatsian third line of 'A Clan Gathering' is quoted from
Kit Wright's poem 'Advice for Attending a Hundredth Birthday
Party'. 'Re-entering the Egg' is dedicated to Róisín Bryce.